Sports Illustrated KIDS

HOCKEY RECORDS SMASHED!

by Bruce Berglund

CAPSTONE PRESS
a capstone imprint

Published by Capstone Press, an imprint of Capstone
1710 Roe Crest Drive, North Mankato, Minnesota 56003
capstonepub.com

Library of Congress Cataloging-in-Publication Data
Names: Berglund, Bruce R. author.
Title: Hockey records smashed! / by Bruce Berglund.
Description: North Mankato, Minnesota : Capstone Press, [2024] | Series: Sports illustrated kids. Record smashers | Includes bibliographical references and index. | Audience: Ages 9–11 | Audience: Grades 4–6 | Summary: "In hockey, the fast play and fierce competition make for some spectacular feats on the ice—like Sarah Nurse's remarkable Olympic play in 2022 and the Montreal Canadiens' unmatchable Stanley Cup wins. In this Sports Illustrated Kids book, young readers can witness record-breaking moments in hockey. Fast-paced and fact-filled, this collection of record smashers will delight sports fans with thrilling achievements in hockey history"—Provided by publisher.
Identifiers: LCCN 2023003518 (print) | LCCN 2023003519 (ebook) | ISBN 9781669050117 (hardcover) | ISBN 9781669071594 (paperback) | ISBN 9781669050070 (pdf) | ISBN 9781669050094 (kindle edition) | ISBN 9781669050100 (epub)
Subjects: LCSH: Hockey—Records—Juvenile literature. | Hockey—History—Juvenile literature.
Classification: LCC GV847.25 .B439 2024 (print) | LCC GV847.25 (ebook) | DDC 796.356—dc23/eng/20230209
LC record available at https://lccn.loc.gov/2023003518
LC ebook record available at https://lccn.loc.gov/2023003519

Editorial Credits
Editor: Ericka Smith; Designer: Terri Poburka; Media Researcher: Svetlana Zhurkin; Production Specialist: Katy LaVigne

Image Credits
Alamy: Reuters/Gary Hershorn, 28; Associated Press: Isaac Brekken, 11, Petr David Josek, 19; Getty Images: Bettmann, 26, Bruce Bennett, 21, Bruce Bennett Studios, 29, Elsa, 5, 14, 20, Freestyle Photography/Jana Chytilova, 6, Graig Abel, 27, Jim McIsaac, 15, NHLI/Andre Ringuette, 7, 8, 9, NHLI/Dave Reginek, 12, NHLI/Denis Brodeur, 25, NHLI/Geoff Burke, 4, NHLI/Scott Rovak, 17, Paul Bereswill, 16, Richard Heathcote, 18, Rob Carr, 10; Shutterstock: krissikunterbunt (fireworks), cover and throughout, pixssa (cracked background), 1 and throughout, Ruslan Shevchenko, cover (back), Tino Bandito, 22; Sports Illustrated: Simon Bruty, cover (front), Tony Triolo, 23

Printed and bound in the USA. 5425

TABLE OF CONTENTS

Words in **bold** are in the glossary.

THE COOLEST RECORDS

Hockey is a game of speed and skill. Players fire laser passes across the ice. They fly down the rink. They stickhandle past defenders. And goalies kick their legs across the net to stop shots.

It's exciting when our favorite hockey teams win. It's even more exciting when players smash records!

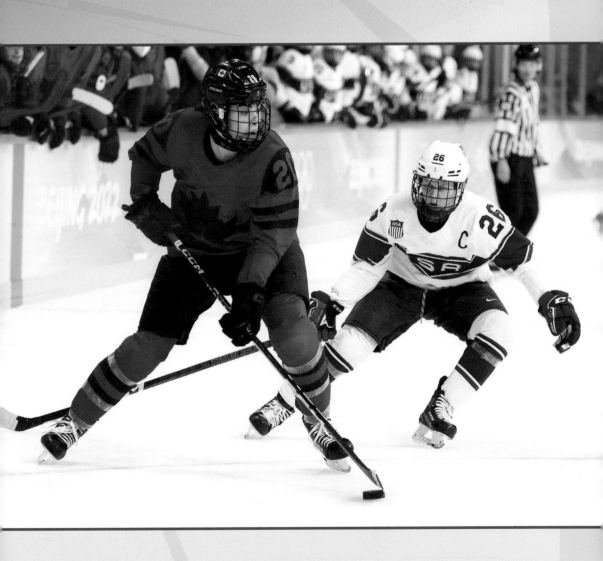

RECORD-SETTING START

It's unusual for a **rookie** in the National Hockey League (NHL) to set a record during his first game. But that's what Auston Matthews did.

Auston Matthews

Matthews scored a goal in the first period.
A few minutes later, he scored again.

Matthews scoring his first goal in the NHL

In the second period, he got a third goal. Then, with just seconds left in the second period, he scored his fourth goal. It was a new record! Four NHL rookies had scored three goals in their first game. No one had scored four in the NHL's modern era—since 1943.

Matthews after his third goal

Matthews with the four pucks he used to score his four goals

FACT

When a player scores three goals in a game, it's called a "hat trick." In NHL arenas, fans throw hats onto the ice when a player scores a hat trick.

OVERTIME THREAT

Alex Ovechkin has scored many goals. He's especially good at scoring **clutch** goals. When the Capitals need a win, Ovechkin delivers.

In 2017, the Capitals were playing the Red Wings. At the end of the third period, the score was tied 3–3. The game went into overtime.

Alex Ovechkin (left)

Ovechkin celebrates a game-winning goal with his teammates.

Ovechkin scored and won the game. It was his 20th winning goal in overtime. He smashed Jaromir Jagr's record of 19 overtime goals!

NHL Players with the Most Career Overtime Goals

Player	Years Played	Overtime Goals
Alex Ovechkin	2005–2022	24
Sidney Crosby	2005–2022	19
Jaromir Jagr	1990–2018	19

THE WINNINGEST GOALIE

No NHL goalie has won more games than Martin Brodeur. In 2009, he was in his 15th season with the New Jersey Devils. When they beat the Blackhawks, he had 552 wins. He smashed Patrick Roy's record!

Martin Brodeur

Brodeur played six more seasons. He finished his career with 691 wins. No other NHL goalie has won even 600 games.

Brodeur also holds the NHL record for most career shutouts. In 125 games, he kept the other team from scoring any goals.

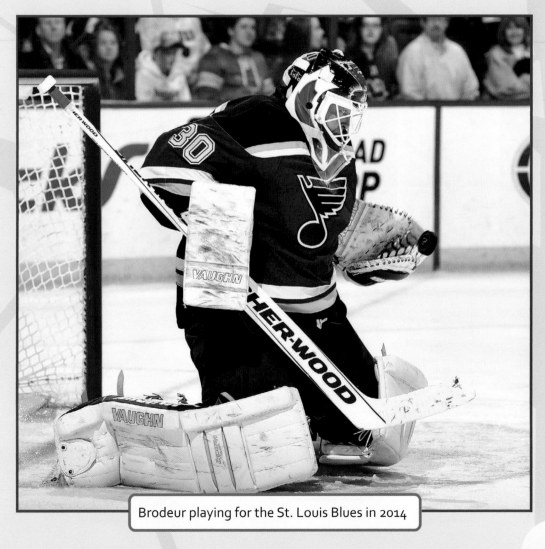

Brodeur playing for the St. Louis Blues in 2014

OLYMPIC SCORER

When the 2022 gold-medal game between Canada and the United States began, Canada's Sarah Nurse was two points away from making history. Hayley Wickenheiser had held the record for the most total points in one Olympic hockey **tournament**. Wickenheiser had made 5 goals and 12 **assists**—17 points.

Sarah Nurse

Hayley Wickenheiser

In the first period, Nurse scored a goal to tie the record. In the second period, she assisted on a goal. That gave Nurse 5 goals and 13 assists. She smashed Wickenheiser's record!

Nurse (left) celebrating after scoring a goal during the 2022 gold-medal game

CUP WINNERS

The biggest prize in the NHL is the Stanley Cup. Hockey teams first competed for the cup in 1893. Since then, one team has won the prize more than any other—the Montreal Canadiens.

The Stanley Cup

The Canadiens (in white) playing against the Flyers in the 1976 Stanley Cup Finals

More than once, the Canadiens had a great **dynasty**. The team would win the championship year after year. Once the team won the Stanley Cup five years in a row. In total, they have a whopping 24 wins!

Today, NHL teams are more evenly matched. It's harder for a team to win year after year. The Canadiens' record won't likely be beat.

Teams with the Most Stanley Cup Wins

Team	Stanley Cup Wins
Montreal Canadiens	24
Toronto Maple Leafs	13
Detroit Red Wings	11
Boston Bruins	6
Chicago Blackhawks	6
Edmonton Oilers	5
Pittsburgh Penguins	5

The Canadiens celebrating their 1993 Stanley Cup win

GRETZKY'S GREATEST RECORD

Hockey's best record smasher is Wayne Gretzky. Before Gretzky, the record for most goals in a season was 76. In 1982, he scored 92. Before Gretzky, the record for most points in a season was 152. In 1986, he smashed that record with 215 points.

Wayne Gretzky

In 1989, Gretzky smashed the record for most career points. Gordie Howe held the old record of 1,850 points. Howe had played for 26 seasons. Gretzky broke Howe's record in just 11 seasons!

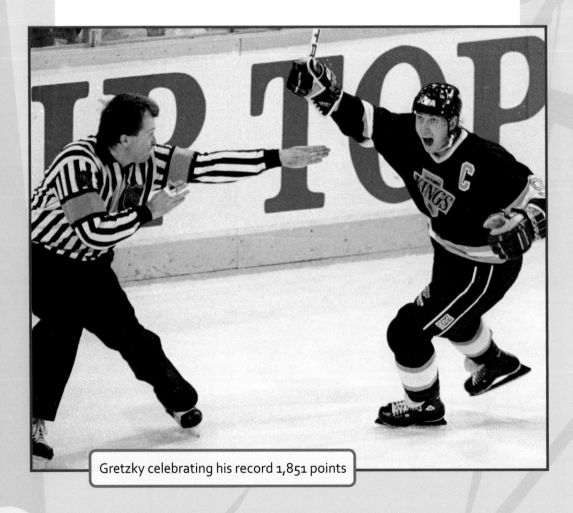

Gretzky celebrating his record 1,851 points

Gretzky (left) and Howe celebrate Gretzky's new record

FACT

A player's total points are their goals added with their assists. After his final season in 1999, Gretzky had 2,857 total points. If you took away his 894 goals, his 1,963 assists would still give him the most total points of any NHL player.

GLOSSARY

assist (uh-SIST)—a pass that leads to a score by a teammate

clutch (KLUHCH)—made late in the game to help one's team win the game

dynasty (DYE-nuh-stee)—a team that wins two or more championships year after year

rookie (RUK-ee)—a player who is playing their first year on a team

tournament (TUR-nuh-muhnt)—a series of matches between several players or teams, ending in one winner

READ MORE

Flynn, Brendan. *Basketball Records Smashed!*
North Mankato, MN: Capstone, 2024.

Smith, Elliott. *Hockey's Greatest Myths and Legends.*
North Mankato, MN: Capstone, 2023.

Walker, Tracy Sue. *Wayne Gretzky: The Great One.*
Minneapolis: Lerner Publications, 2023.

INTERNET SITES

DK Find Out!: Ice Hockey
dkfindout.com/us/sports/ice-hockey

Hockey Hall of Fame: Hockeypedia
hhof.com/hockeypedia/hockeypedia.html

Hockey Reference: NHL Leaders & Records
hockey-reference.com/leaders

INDEX

ABOUT THE AUTHOR

Bruce Berglund played baseball, hockey, and football as a kid. When he got older, he was a coach and referee. Bruce taught college history for many years. He wrote a history book for adults on world hockey. He is now writing a book about the history of referees and umpires.